W9-BGR-518

MOVING ON

SENIOR AUTHORS

Virginia A. Arnold   Carl B. Smith

LITERATURE CONSULTANTS

Joan I. Glazer   Margaret H. Lippert

Macmillan Publishing Company
New York

Collier Macmillan Publishers
London

ACKNOWLEDGMENTS

The publisher gratefully acknowledges permission to reprint the following copyrighted material:

"How Big?" from OUT IN THE DARK AND DAYLIGHT by Aileen Fisher. Copyright © 1980 by Aileen Fisher. By permission of Harper & Row, Publishers, Inc.

"Sitting in the Sand" from DOGS & DRAGONS, TREES & DREAMS: A Collection of Poems by Karla Kuskin. Copyright © 1958 by Karla Kuskin. By permission of Harper & Row, Publishers, Inc.

"Tugs" from I GO A-TRAVELING by James S. Tippett. Copyright © 1929 by Harper & Row, Publishers, Inc.; renewed 1957 by James S. Tippett. By permission of Harper & Row, Publishers, Inc.

"Where the Sun Lives" a folk tale based on the story *How the Sun Was Brought Back to the Sky* by Mirra Ginsburg by permission of the author and publisher, Macmillan Publishing Company.

ILLUSTRATION CREDITS: Amy Schwartz, 4-13; Bob Shein, 14-21; Allan Eitzen, 22-29; Mac Evans, 30-31; Linda Solovic, 32-33, 68-69; Jerry Smath, 34-41; Saul Mandel, 42-43; Gary Zamchick, 44-53; François Caumartin and Julie Garneau, 54-65; Higgins Bond, 66-67; Gayla Godell, 70-79.

PHOTO CREDITS: Photo, Francis G. Mayer, 10. © Lawrence Migdale, 15-21. The Metropolitan Museum of Art, Harris Brisbane Dick Fund, 1956. CAT, Egyptian, Late Dynastic, Ptolemaic period. Bronze, H. 28cm, 11. Wolfe Fund, 1907. Catherine Lorillard Wolfe Collection, *Mme. Charpentier and Her Children*. Pierre August Renoir, 1878, oil on canvas, 12.

Copyright © 1987 Macmillan Publishing Company, a division of Macmillan, Inc.

All rights reserved. No part of this book may be reproduced or transmitted in any form or by any means, electronic or mechanical, including photocopying, recording, or by any information storage and retrieval system, without permission in writing from the Publisher.

Macmillan Publishing Company
866 Third Avenue
New York, N.Y. 10022
Collier Macmillan Canada, Inc.

Printed in the United States of America

ISBN 0-02-163630-3

9 8 7 6 5 4 3

Contents
Level 3, MOVING ON

A Ride on

the Bus

Anne Rockwell

Kate and Sam like to go to the city.
Kate and Sam like to see Grandmother.
Grandmother likes to see Kate and Sam.

Kate likes to ride the bus in the city.
"May Sam and I take a ride on this bus?"
Kate says.

"Where can this bus go, Grandmother?"
says Sam.

"This bus can take you to a pet show," says Grandmother.

"I like pets," says Kate.
"Come on!"

"Where is the pet show?" says Sam.

"Come with me and you can see," says Grandmother.

"Look at the pets!" says Kate.
"I see a pony.
I wish I could ride on the pony."

"You can look at the pony.
You can't ride on it," says Grandmother.

"This cat is not like my cat," says Sam.
"It can't live with me.
It can't play with me.
What can it do?"

"This cat can sit and look at you,"
says Grandmother.

"Do you like the dog?"
says Grandmother.

"I can't see a dog," says Sam.

"I can. I can see a dog," says Kate.
"I wish this dog could live with me."

"I like the pets in this show," says Sam.

"It is time to go!" says Grandmother.

"Where can Sam and I go now?" says Kate.
"I like to ride the bus in the city."

"I wish I could live in the city!" says Sam.

STOP AND GO

WAY

Anne Rockwell

"I wish Mary and I could go to the 9
park now," says Lin. 13

"I can take you now," says Mother. 20
"Get in the car. 24
I can stop and pick up Mary." 31

Mother and Lin pick up Mary. 37

15

"I can read and ride," says Lin.
"Look, Mother!
It says STOP."

Mother stops to look.
"Now I can go."

"I see a red light," says Mary. *64*

Mother stops the car at the red light. *82*

"You stop at the red light and go *90* on the green," says Mary. *95*

⑰

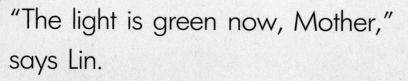

"The light is green now, Mother,"
says Lin.
"You can go.
Mary, what do you like to play in the park?"

"I like to play *Red Light, Green Light*,"
says Mary.

Mother sees a bus with boys and girls in it.
The red light on the bus says STOP.
Mother stops the car.

"Now the boys and girls can get out and walk,"
says Mary.

ONE W

"I see the park!" says Lin.

"Now you can park the car."

Mother, Lin, and Mary get out and walk.

"Stop and look at the light," says Mother.

"You walk on green and stop on red," says Lin.

"The light is green," says Mary.

"It says WALK," Lin says.

"Come on!" says Mary.
"Come and play *Red Light, Green Light*
with me!"

Little Tugs Help Big Boats

Anne Rockwell

The sun is up in the city.
Boats come and go on the water.
The little red boat is a tug.
Jan is on the tug with Daddy.

That big boat can't go. 33

The little boat can help the big boat.

It can tug the big boat. 47

Now that big boat can go. 53

It can go where the little boat tugs it. 62

The little tug can push big boats, too. 70

That big boat is too big to get in. 79

With help, it can get in. 85

The little tug can help it. 91

The tug can push the big boat in. 99

25

Jan likes to ride with Daddy on the tug.
She likes to help Daddy.
Daddy likes to help Jan, too.

Jan sees the sun go down.
At night, the big boats can't see the little boat.
It is time to light up the boat.
Jan and Daddy put on a red light and a green light.
The red light and the green light help the big boats see the little tug.

Little tugs
help
big boats.

Now it is night.

It is time to go in.

The tug can't push boats at night.

Jan and Daddy go in and sit down.

Jan likes to read to Daddy.

That book is on boats.

It says LITTLE TUGS HELP BIG BOATS.

Daddy likes the book that Jan did.

TUGS

Chug! Puff! Chug!
Push, little tug.
Push the great ship here
Close to its pier.

Chug! Puff! Chug!
Pull, strong tug.
Drawing all alone
Three boat-loads of stone.

Busy harbor tugs,
Like round water bugs,
Hurry here and there,
Working everywhere.

James S. Tippett

SKILLS activity

Short Vowels

Hear	Read	Write
	b<u>u</u>s car	<u>bus</u>

 city   stop   1. _____

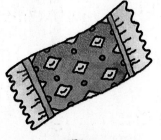 tug   go   2. _____

that   jump   3. _____

 red   Lin   4. _____

Read	Write
i u I like the c___ty.	I like the city.

i u 1. Ned and Ann l___ve in the city.

i u 2. Ned and Ann take a b___s.

u i 3. Ned and Ann f___sh in the water.

i u 4. Ned and Ann see the t___gs.

u i 5. The l___ttle tugs push big boats.

The Giant Man
and the
Giant Woman

Jerry Smath

A little cat and a little dog live *8*
in a little home. *12*
The little home is in a little city. *20*

The little city is on the water. *27*
In the water live a giant man *34*
and a giant woman. *38*

The little cat and dog like the giant man 47
and the giant woman. 51
The giant man and the giant woman like 59
the little cat and dog. 64

The little cat and dog like to ride in a boat.
The giant man and the giant woman
like to tug the boat.

"Look at the boat go up and down,"
says the giant man.

"Look at the water," says the little cat.
"Look at it go up and up.
It will get to the little city.
What can we do?
Help! Help!"

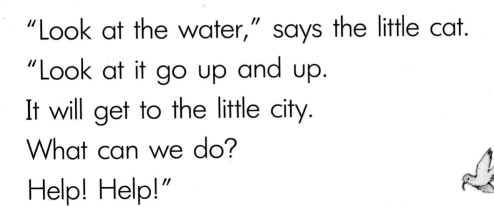

"We can help you,"
says the giant woman.
"We can drink the water.
We can drink and drink."

"Look!" says the little dog.
"Look at the water go down and down."

"You did help," says the little cat
to the giant man and the giant woman.
"Now we can go home.
We can go home to the little city."

Sitting in the Sand

Sitting in the sand and the sea comes up 9
So you put your hands together 15
And you use them like a cup 22
And you dip them in the water 29
With a scooping kind of motion 35
And before the sea goes out again 42
You have a sip of ocean. 48

Karla Kuskin

FLY TO THE MOON

Virginia A. Arnold

Tim and Jenny like to play 6
in the park. 9
Tim looks out. 12
He says, "I wish we could 18
go out and play." 22

"But the sun is not out," 28
says Jenny. 30
"We can't go out and play, 36
but we can play at home." 42

45

"We can play *Fly To The Moon*," 49
says Jenny. 51
"We can help this man get to the moon." 61

Tim reads. 63
"Push Ⓐ," he says. 67

"Look! We did help the man fly 74
to the moon," says Tim.

"The man can fly very quickly,"
says Jenny.

Tim reads.

"What can you do on the moon?" he says.

"You can jump on the moon," says Jenny.
"I push A ."

Tim looks at the man.

He says, "On the moon you can take
a very big jump.
Look at that man jump up!"

Jenny reads.

"What can't you do on the moon?" she says.

"You can't grow seeds on the moon," says Tim.
"I push B."

Jenny looks at the man.

"Look!" she says.

"You can't grow seeds, but you can walk
on the moon."

"I wish we could fly to the moon,"
says Jenny.

Tim looks out.
"We can't fly to the moon," he says.

"But we can walk to the park,"
says Jenny.
"The sun is out now."

Jenny and Tim walk to the park.
"I can take a very big jump," Tim says.
"Look at me!"

"What a big jump," says Jenny.
"You can jump like that man
on the moon!"

WHERE THE

an adaptation of a folk tale by Mirra Ginsburg

SUN LIVES

For days and days the sun did not 8
light up the sky. 12
"Where did the sun go?" says the little cat. 21
"I will go and look for the sun." 29

"Do you know where the sun lives?" 36
says the mother cat. 40

"I do not know where it lives," 47
says the little cat. 51
"I will look for it." 56

The little cat walks to the dog. *63*

"Do you know where the sun lives?" *70*

says the cat. *73*

"I do not know, but the pony may know," *82*

says the dog. *85*

The cat and the dog walk to the pony.
"Do you know where the sun lives?"
says the dog.

"I do not know, but the bird may know,"
says the pony.

The cat, the dog, and the pony walk
to the bird.
"Do you know where the sun lives?"
says the pony.

"I do not know, but the moon will know,"
says the bird.

The cat, the dog, the pony, and the bird
fly to the moon.
"Do you know where the sun lives?"
says the bird.

"I do know where the sun lives,"
the moon says.
"I will take you to the sun."

"This is where the sun lives," says the moon.
"The sun lives in the sky!"

"Where is it?" the cat says.
"I can't see it."

"I can see the sun," says the pony.
"You can't sleep now, Sun.
It is time to get up!"

"I can't get up now," says the sun.
"Look at me.
I can't light up that sky.
I will go to sleep now.
I will sleep for days and days."

"We can help you," says the bird.
"We will help you light up the sky.
Get up now."
The cat, the dog, the pony, and the bird
did help the sun.

"Now you can light up the sky!"
says the bird.

"Now I will help you," the sun says.
"I will light up the sky for you!"

"The sun is out!" says the dog.
"It is light."

"Now we can go home," says the cat.
"We know where the sun lives.
It lives in the sky!"

How Big?

The sun, they say, is very big,
a star that shines by day,
much bigger than the whole big earth,
oh, very much, they say.

But when I'm hiding in a field
of clover-smelling hay,
a single little clover plant
can hide the sun away.

Aileen Fisher

Initial Consonants

Hear	Read	Write
	down <u>f</u>or	<u>for</u>

   moon   night   1. _____

   home   giant   2. _____

   you   walks   3. _____

did   seeds   4. _____

Read	Write
k s̲ The __un is out.	The sun is out.

l r 1. It __ooks like a man.

c z 2. It __an light up the sky.

p d 3. We will __ush the little car.

n t 4. You can't see it at __ight.

g t 5. It is __ime to sleep.

Picture Dictionary

B b

boat

The <u>boat</u> is in the water.

boats

<u>Boats</u> come to the city.

bus

Boys and girls ride on the <u>bus</u>.

but

A fish can swim, <u>but</u> it can't walk.

C c

car

Father and the boys take a ride in the <u>car</u>.

city

Jane and Jeff live in the <u>city</u>.

D d

days

We will ride on the boat for <u>days</u> and <u>days</u>.

drink

My dog, my cat, and I <u>drink</u> water.

F f

fly

A bird can <u>fly</u>, and you can <u>fly</u>, too.

G g

giant

This bird is a <u>giant</u> bird.

grandmother

"I like to go to see my <u>grandmother</u>," says Jan.

green

This is a <u>green</u> house.

H h

he

Ted likes the book, and <u>he</u> reads it to Jenny.

home

I live in a big <u>home</u>.
A bird lives in a little <u>home</u>.

K k

know

We <u>know</u> where the cat is.

light

Nan and Pam put a <u>light</u> on at night.

live

Fish <u>live</u> in the water.

lives

Jane <u>lives</u> on a boat with Mother and Father.

looks

Carlos <u>looks</u> like Ted.

man

The <u>man</u> is too big to ride the little pony.

moon

We can see the <u>moon</u> at night.

P p

pets

My <u>pets</u> and I like to walk in the park.

push

The boys <u>push</u> the little car.

reads

Jim <u>reads</u> the time on the clock.

red

The bird is <u>red</u>.

S s

sky

What can you see in the <u>sky</u>?

sleep

We <u>sleep</u> at night.

stop

Ann and Ben <u>stop</u> to look at the pony.

stops

Kate <u>stops</u> at the red light.

T t

that

This man looks like <u>that</u> man.

too

Ben can read, and Nan can read, <u>too</u>.

T t

tug

A <u>tug</u> is a little boat that can help big boats.

tugs

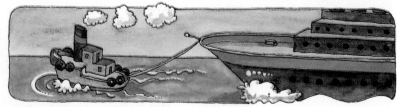

The little boat <u>tugs</u> the big boat.

V v

very

The moon looks <u>very</u> big.

W w

walk

Ned and Jan <u>walk</u> home.

we

Sam and I know where <u>we</u> can get the bus.

where

"<u>Where</u> will this bus stop?" says Kate.

will

We <u>will</u> wait for the bus to come.

woman

The <u>woman</u> will help the girls.

Word List

To the teacher: The following words are introduced in *Moving On*. The page number to the left of a word indicates where the word first appears in the selection.

Instructional-Vocabulary words are printed in black. Words printed in red are Applied Skills words that children should be able to decode independently, using previously taught phonics skills.

A Ride on the Bus
5. bus
6. city
   Grandmother
7. where
8. pets
11. live

Stop and Go
14. stop
15. car
16. stops
17. red
   green
   light
19. walk

Little Tugs Help Big Boats
22. tugs
   boats
23. tug
   boat
24. that
25. push
   too

The Giant Man and the Giant Woman
34. giant
   woman
   man
35. home
39. we
40. drink

Fly to the Moon
44. fly
   moon
45. but
   he
   looks
46. reads
47. very

Where the Sun Lives
55. lives
   days
   will
   sky
56. know
61. sleep

7.61